THE ILLUSTRATED WORLD OF

THE ILLUSTRATED WORLD OF

Megan Hess

Hardie Grant

BOOKS

For Martina Granolic

Couture is utterly original and
truly inspiring, just like you.

Introduction / 09

01 THE CREATORS [19]
02 THE COLLECTORS [47]
03 THE DRAMA [81]
04 THE DETAILS [121]
05 THE CITIES [145]
06 THE INSPIRATION [177]

Acknowledgements / 220
About the author / 223

INTRODUCTION

It was a single dress that kindled my interest in the world of haute couture. I was young at the time, maybe eleven or twelve, and I knew nothing of the designers, seasons and runway shows of high fashion. But as I sat watching the opening scenes of *Breakfast at Tiffany's*, I was transfixed by Audrey Hepburn. I knew instinctively that the black gown she was wearing, with its chic high neck and elegant but unusual back perfectly cut away at the shoulder blades, must have been made by someone special.

It was the first time I'd even considered who actually made the clothes I saw every day, and the realisation lit a spark. When I discovered it was the inimitable couturier Hubert Givenchy who had designed the iconic look, and that the dress had been created specifically for Hepburn herself, I was captivated. I knew that somehow I wanted gorgeous, hand-stitched, custom-designed clothes to feature in my life too.

Fast forward to now, and I am lucky enough to work in the rarefied world I once marvelled at as a girl. My illustrations have given me access to places only a few ever get to see. I've visited invitation-only ateliers and attended fashion shows that have given me shivers. Never in a million years did I think I'd ever get to sketch couture at Cannes Film Festival or see the Chanel métiers d'arts up close. But ever since that first time I gazed in awe at that simple but exquisite dress worn by Hepburn as Holly Golightly, I've well and truly fallen in love with fashion's premier artform.

This book is my celebration of everything haute couture. It is part collection of my favourite couture moments and part exploration of the most fascinating facets of couture. Most of all it is my love letter to this fairytale industry.

Yes, couture is an exclusive world, hard to gain entry into and filled with unspoken rules and secret languages. But appreciating it is definitely not out of reach. One of the true joys of fashion is getting swept up in couture's creativity, its luxury, its unyielding commitment to excellence, and of course its impossible beauty.

In this book, we'll discover that couture is about so much more than the clothes. It is about the theatre of the runway shows, the age-old techniques and craftsmanship, the fantasies created from the most surprising inspirations, and the people who design, make and wear it. We will learn about the skills developed in couture ateliers over the last century: the hours of painstaking beading, the rare feathers, the intricate embroidery and delicate pleats made by hand. We will journey to my favourite fashion cities and encounter some of the collectors of couture pieces. And throughout the book, I'll introduce you to some of couture's most-loved designers and show you how they became master couturiers.

The world of couture, once you start to look, is endlessly enchanting. By the time you've made it through these pages, I am sure you will agree.

Enjoy!

Megan Hess

FOR *every dress* SENT DOWN THE RUNWAY, THERE ARE A HUNDRED *behind-the-scenes* ELEMENTS COMING TOGETHER WITH *precision-perfect* HARMONY.

HAUTE COUTURE

NOUN, FRENCH: 'HIGH FASHION'

The couture collection for any design house is its premier offering. Shown just twice a year, Spring-Summer and Autumn-Winter, these collections represent the pinnacle of fashion.

Technically, to be couture is to be one-of-a-kind, made by hand and to measure for an individual client. It is in contrast to pret-a-porter, or ready-to-wear, which can be reproduced multiple times in standard sizes and purchased off the rack.

True haute couture, though, is more than just intricate clothes made to measure by hand. It is actually an exclusive designation protected by law and regulated by a governing body in the home of fashion, France.

In order to receive certification and call their work haute couture, a house must be officially invited onto the schedule at Paris Fashion Week by the couture arm of the Fédération de la Haute Couture et de la Mode: the Chambre Syndicale de la Haute Couture. There are only two dozen or so designers invited each year and half of those are there only as guests. Full members must have an atelier in France, but correspondent membership is offered to some foreign houses.

The Chambre Syndicale has strict rules for what constitutes haute couture. To even be considered, a house must create two made-to-measure collections a year, each with a minimum number of looks. They must have a certain number of staff and maintain an atelier in Paris where they offer private fittings for clients.

The full set of rules have never been made public, but the Chambre Syndicale did once release a delightfully mysterious list of five requirements such as 'excellence in handmade and tailor-made production' and 'participation in parades of the profession'. The final requirement? *Permanence de ces engagements* – 'permanence of these commitments'. Couture is made to last a lifetime, or maybe many lifetimes, so it seems fitting that there is an expectation for couture houses to uphold standards season after season.

CHAMBRE SYNDICALE *de la* HAUTE COUTURE

01

Conception de la collection par un créateur permanent
Collection design by a permanent designer

02

Excellence de la réalisation fait main et sur mesure au sein de l'entreprise
Excellence in handmade and tailor-made production within the company

03

Taille minimale de l'entreprise
Minimum business size

04

Participation aux défilés de la profession
Participation in parades of the profession

05

Permanence de ces engagements
Permanence of these commitments

Chapter 01

THE CREATORS

Often when we consider the creators of couture, we immediately think of the designers who lead each house. But if the concept comes from an inspired head designer, the execution is a labour of love. Each piece in a couture collection takes hundreds of hours of work by many different people to create.

All haute couture houses have their own distinctive signature, and a great designer takes cues from the traditions they're working with and infuses them with their own DNA. They may take inspiration from wide and varied sources, but there are recognisable flourishes in all their creations. Gothic Victorianism and military-style jackets – perfectly Alexander McQueen. Pearls, camellias and cropped bouclé jackets – quintessentially Chanel. Exploded tulle and voluminous ruffled skirts – distinctively Giambattista Valli.

To truly understand couture, we need to meet all of the people in the atelier that take couture from idea to runway, red carpet or soiree, and see how the history that filters down through generations of couturiers is like a language that evolves over time.

THE
HEAD DESIGNER

Often just as recognisable as the famous clients they dress, the head designer is without doubt the creative force behind every couture house. The designer sketches their ideas or uses muslin to drape and cut into an early version of the garment. Large teams of seamstresses and artisans then work from these drawings or templates to bring the final piece to life.

These master couturiers understand figure and form like no one else. Most have been apprenticed in the traditions and craftsmanship of couture for years before they head their own house. They are highly attuned to the history of fashion, but at the same time they must be innovative enough to bring something new to every collection. To design clothes that conjure a dream and transport people into a different realm takes singular vision.

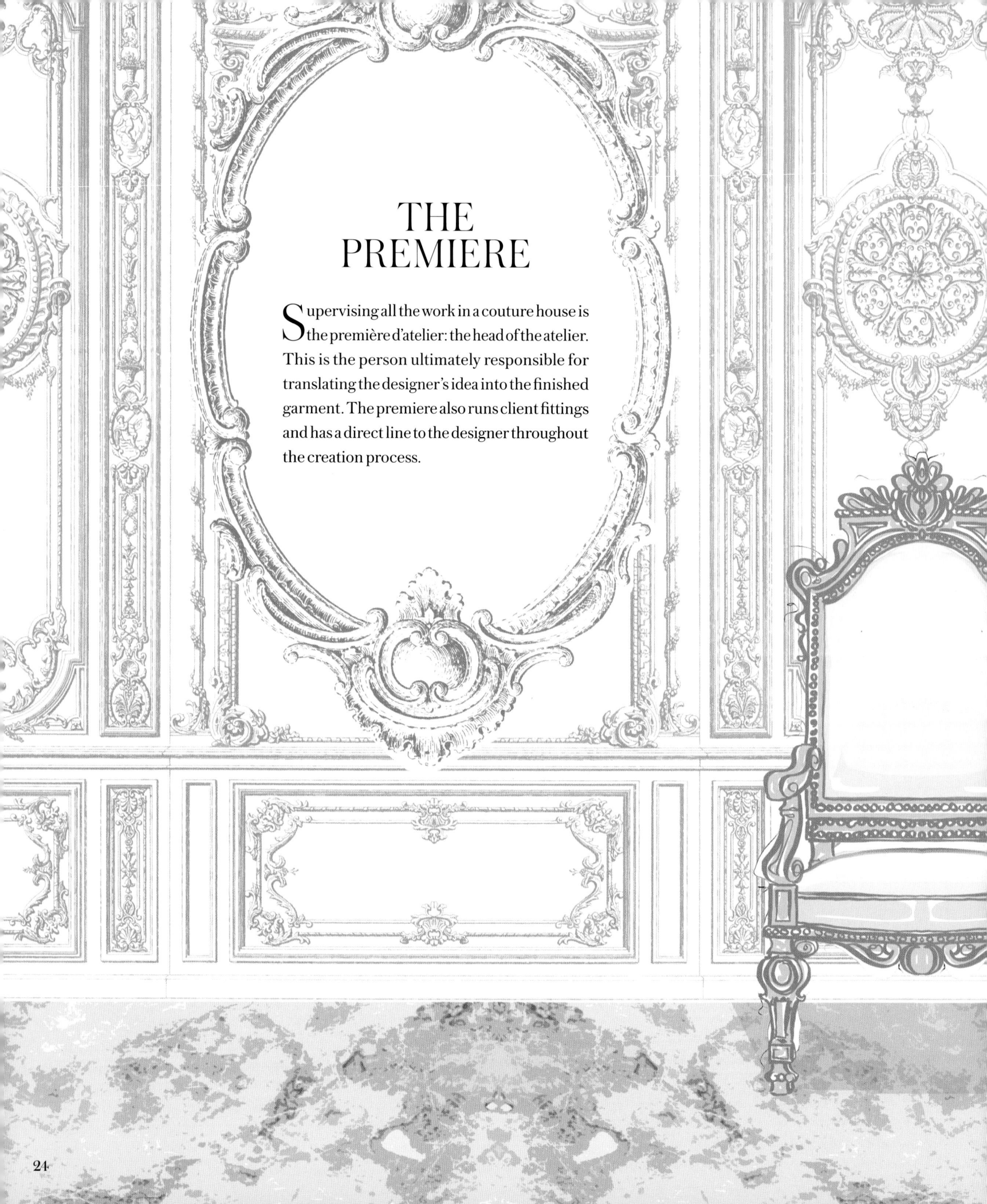

THE PREMIERE

Supervising all the work in a couture house is the première d'atelier: the head of the atelier. This is the person ultimately responsible for translating the designer's idea into the finished garment. The premiere also runs client fittings and has a direct line to the designer throughout the creation process.

THE PETITES MAINS

The 'little hands' of couture are the seamstresses who bring couture to life. Instantly recognisable in their iconic uniform of white coats with measuring tapes around their necks and pins between their teeth, they are the foundation of the entire industry.

The petites mains are highly skilled and revered for the painstaking work they do behind the scenes. It is in the hands of these seamstresses that a master couturier trusts his or her designs to be executed without a single stitch out of place. Toiling away quietly in an atelier may not sound like the most glamourous side of couture, but to watch these talented tailors draping, cutting, pressing and hand-stitching with such complete focus and care is to see ordinary materials become works of art.

'*Couture* IS A SPACE WHERE YOU CAN DESIGN THE HOUSE *for your body the way you want* – WITH THE HELP OF THE DESIGNER, THE TEAM AND THE ATELIERS.'

– MARIA GRAZIA CHIURI

PATTERN MAKERS

FLAT PATTERN CUTTER

A talented pattern cutter is like gold in a couture atelier. Once a design has been sketched by a designer, it is the pattern cutter's job to translate it into a flat pattern using incredible spatial awareness and understanding of construction. Pattern cutting tools – drafting paper, pencils, scissors and innumerable rulers, set squares and protractors – can make these specialists seem more like engineers or architects than seamstresses. The resulting patterns are marvels of interpretation: both of the initial design sketch and of the measurements and contours of the human body.

DRAPER

Draping is part of the pattern making for some designs. It is also an art unto itself. A seamstress, pattern cutter or designer takes the fabric the final piece will be made in and lays it across a mannequin, pinning each section as he or she goes. In a way the draper is creating a three-dimensional pattern, letting the fall of fabric itself dictate how the final garment should be constructed.

TOOLS OF THE TRADE

MANNEQUIN

Step inside any seamstress's workshop and you're bound to see half-dressed mannequins dotted amongst the tables of fabric. At a couture atelier, these aren't just any mannequins: each will have been made for one particular client, to exactly her measurements. It is tradition that a client is bequeathed a single mannequin for her entire life. These precise models are used between personal fittings to ensure a garment always fits like a glove. Its size and shape may change as the years pass – growing or shrinking as we all inevitably do – but it will remain forever hers. If you're ever in a position to see these mannequins at work, don't for a second expect you'll know which famous client is getting which piece. Ownership is usually designated only by a discreet number, preserving the mystery from any prying eyes.

TOILE

An early version of a garment made of linen or calico, a toile is a prototype used to see how construction techniques, pattern measurements and embellishment placement will work before a single inch of the precious silk, delicate tulle or hand-crafted lace is sacrificed. Toiles are made almost universally in white or cream, often with paper embellishments pinned to them to show embroidery or beading, and they offer a fabulous insight into the creation process. If you peer closely at a toile, you'll likely see tiny notes and markings from pattern makers and seamstresses as they communicate what works and what doesn't.

THE FIT MODELS

Beyond the actual creators there are myriad supporting roles that take couture from the workshops to the runways. One that is vital but almost never spoken about is the in-house fit model. Like a living, breathing mannequin – one with the posture of a ballerina and patience of a saint – the in-house fit model tries on each piece that is destined for a show and stands uncomplainingly still as the petites mains redrape, repleat, resew and recut to ensure everything is perfect. Chanel's in-house fit model, Amanda Sanchez, has worked for the house for nearly two decades and a huge number of their iconic designs have been made exactly to her proportions – what a job!

THE MÉTIERS D'ART

Alongside the atelier staff employed directly by designers are the independent artisans with highly specialised skills: the métiers d'art. These suppliers, sometimes also called 'fournisseurs', are devoted to rare trades that require incredibly technical knowledge and are central to the very idea of couture.

Many of the métiers d'art have been collaborating with the likes of Dior, Chanel and Givenchy for decades, and they may serve multiple couture houses. In their workshops, each intricate detail is lovingly hand-crafted, then packaged up in tissue and couriered across town to be incorporated into final garments by the petites mains.

The contribution of métiers d'art to this fabulous artform cannot be overstated. It is not unheard of that a sample from an embroiderer or a lacemaker will inspire an entire collection. We'll find out more about these specific makers in the Details chapter.

FEATURE DESIGNER

MEMBER CHAMBRE SYNDICALE DE LA HAUTE COUTURE SINCE 1947
30 AVENUE MONTAIGNE, PARIS

You can't talk about the creators of couture without mentioning Dior. The house has been home to so many incredible designers over its seventy-year history, from Christian Dior himself to Yves Saint Laurent and John Galliano, right through to current creative director Maria Grazia Chiuri.

A couturier at Dior doesn't follow the zeitgeist, they define it – a legacy that began the moment Christian Dior sent his debut couture collection, later dubbed the 'New Look', out into the world in 1947. For years before the New Look hit the scene, women in Europe had been making do with what little they had. World War II had just ended and it was a time of austerity and utilitarianism as women everywhere gave up any small extravagance to help the war effort. The opulent designs that made up Dior's debut collection changed all that overnight.

Dior's luxurious use of fabric, focus on the waist and padded hips caused outrage and controversy, but also started a fashion revolution. The elaborate construction techniques restored the era of glamour and luxury to French fashion and saw a return to the haute couture artisanry that had suffered under the constraints of the war. Every piece was lovingly hand stitched, down to each self-covered button made in the Dior atelier, and the fabrics were heat set to hold their shape.

The New Look – and the Bar suit that was its central pillar – are still some of the most iconic silhouettes in the world. With one collection, Christian Dior completely redefined the fashion of the day. Each designer in the line of Dior successors has put their own stamp on the prestigious maison while following Dior's guiding principle of innovating through fashion.

A NEW LEGACY

'I want to turn couture on its head.'
– JOHN GALLIANO

Christian Dior died unexpectedly of a heart attack in 1957 and his former assistant, Yves Saint Laurent, took over as artistic director. Saint Laurent designed six couture collections for the house before moving on, but in that short time he liberated the Dior look while maintaining a strong connection to his mentor's vision. At only twenty-one, he was the youngest couturier in the world at the time, but that didn't stop him from infusing the codes of Dior with his own bohemian takes.

Saint Laurent radically altered hemlines with each collection, despite the unspoken rule against moving them more than two inches in a single season, and constantly reinvented Christian Dior's famous silhouettes. Saint Laurent's last collection for the house, the 'Beat' Autumn-Winter 1960 collection, foreshadowed the short-skirted, sleeveless and straight-lined fashions of the coming decade. It was a divisive departure from the traditional couture approach.

Years later, in 1996, another famous name took the top job at Dior: John Galliano. As a creator, Galliano pushed the envelope further than most were prepared to – thumbing his nose at the stuffy traditions of haute couture and completing redefining the Dior look once again.

His disregard for social conventions often got him into trouble. His Spring-Summer 2000 couture collection centred around the theme of homelessness, with clothes inspired by the rough sleepers he rode past on his morning commute through Paris. It was described by *WWD* as 'one of the most controversial fashion shows ever staged' and featured silk taffeta printed with newspaper pages and a series of white jackets secured with strings to echo straitjackets. Galliano was eventually let go from the label after controversy in his personal life, but his designs were undeniably imaginative and his sense of theatre was like no other.

MADAME DIOR

Maria Grazia Chiuri was named artistic director at Dior in 2016. Italian-born Chiuri previously spent seventeen years at Valentino working with Pierpaolo Piccioli, her long-time collaborator. As the first female head of Dior in its seventy-year history, she has reimagined the house's notion of femininity.

Her aesthetic is influenced by her identity as a working woman and a mother – she has said her teenage daughter is one of her muses. As such, she is the only artistic director of Dior to have debuted with a ready-to-wear collection instead of couture. Still, in the few years she has been at the helm, she has created some breathtaking couture lines, putting the techniques of couture to work creating clothes suitable for the women of today.

Chiuri's couture brings delicate details to eminently wearable designs: sheer silk net skirts, sunray pleated tulle ruffles and impeccably tailored Bar jackets. Her Spring-Summer 2019 collection offered gowns with corsets made of fabric rather than boning, balancing function with beauty and reinforcing the new Dior philosophy that couture should represent a perfectly comfortable home for her clients to live in.

Beyond the coveted clothes she is creating, Chiuri has also brought an undeniably political voice to Dior. She is leading the charge in fashion's activist era, sending models down the runway in 'We Should All Be Feminists' t-shirts in collaboration with author Chimamanda Ngozi Adichie and commissioning feminist artist Judy Chicago to backdrop her Spring-Summer 2020 couture show with banners that posed questions such as, 'What if women ruled the world?'

But even as Chiuri introduces radical changes, the echoes of the original master remain: the controversy, the challenging of taboos, even her propensity for mostly black collections. After all, it was Christian Dior himself who once declared, 'I could write a book about black.'

'I TRIED TO SHOW THAT *fashion is an art.* FOR THAT, I FOLLOWED THE COUNSEL OF MY MASTER *Christian Dior* AND THE

IMPERISHABLE LESSON OF *Mademoiselle Chanel.* I CREATED FOR MY ERA AND I TRIED TO FORESEE WHAT *tomorrow* WOULD BE.'

– YVES SAINT LAURENT

Chapter
02

THE COLLECTORS

One of the things I get asked about most when I talk about couture is, who is it for? Who actually wears it? And really, I find it such a hard question to answer because in my experience there's no one single type of couture wearer. So many of the women I know who collect couture – and also quite a few men – love it for their own distinct reasons.Couture is high art, deserving of its place alongside priceless paintings and sculptures – and just like any piece of art, the value is in the heart of the collector.

Investing in couture is a way of supporting an industry dedicated to excellence. In return for their patronage, clients get to own a masterpiece that they can hand down through the generations. It's also a chance to experience the process of a true master and wear a piece of clothing designed to flatter exactly your frame. Karl Lagerfeld once told *Vanity Fair* that wearing couture should feel like wearing a t-shirt, albeit one with infinite intricate details and hidden layers.

I've known couture collectors who are doctors, lawyers, scientists – people who you would never imagine had such eye-watering beauty hidden away in their wardrobes. I've also met collectors who wear their couture any chance they get, who revel in the theatre of it and enjoy the self-expression that is possible when wearing something made just for them.

They all share one thing in common: a deep appreciation for the craftsmanship, innovation and creativity that couture represents.

Throughout this chapter you'll hear from a good friend of mine about what draws her to the world of couture. Cathie Reid is an entrepreneur and leader in the fields of healthcare and technology, but her unswerving belief in the power of the right outfit for any occasion has led her to becoming a front row regular of runways around the world.

AN EXCLUSIVE SET

With all the work and vision that goes into couture, the prices are necessarily high. Those lucky enough to own bespoke pieces are often extremely private about their collections. Given the industry is built on its ability to be discreet, this makes for a very mysterious clientele.

The list of couture clients worldwide is closely guarded, but it's said to be around 4000 names long. That's down from 20,000 in the 1950s, the golden age of couture. Some are international shoppers buying outfits to wear at private events and high-society weddings; others are royals for whom clothes are used to make statements in the public eye. Others still are patrons of the arts, buying pieces in order for them to be enjoyed by the whole world in museums and galleries.

Daphne Guinness, one of the best-known couture collectors, owns more than 2500 couture pieces, which she has loaned to the Fashion Institute of Technology. Tatiana Sorokko's collection was shown at the Metropolitan Museum of Art in New York, and countless collectors have loaned pieces to the V&A in London. I for one am so grateful for those who entrust their pieces to displays, sometimes for months on end, so they can be enjoyed by all. Couture houses rely on their generosity when putting on retrospectives and exhibitions, as they rarely hold these one-of-a-kind pieces in their own archives.

INVITATION TO SHOP

In such an exclusive world, even the process of acquiring a piece of couture is shrouded in mystery and ritual. The season begins with the biannual runway presentations in Paris, and just getting to a show is a feat. Invitations are allocated to a select group of fashion editors, industry insiders and patrons. A new or aspiring client needs an entrée – someone who has connections to the house and can request an invitation on their behalf.

As soon as the show begins, the collection is officially open to orders. Some designers insist you buy an entire look, while others are happy to mix and match individual pieces from a collection. Orders often come through via text before the models have even left the runway.

Clients have to be quick to request their favourite looks as designers will rarely sell more than one version of an outfit in the same city or to clients who might move in the same social circles. Larger houses will employ a vendeuse, a highly knowledgeable salesperson to guide clients through their choices. It is up to the vendeuse to keep track of who is ordering what and advise if there's a chance the same look will be seen twice at the one event. Clients can even request global exclusivity on a garment if they so desire.

THE EPITOME OF PERSONALISATION

A COLLECTOR'S PERSPECTIVE

'Couture starts with a conversation, sitting with tea (or champagne!) to discuss the piece that you are interested in and any thoughts you may have on alterations to colour, length or fit to best suit you. The sitting then moves to my least favourite part: having every single part of your body measured and written in a little book. From there a toile is created and a fitting conducted before the garment itself is commenced. The garment is then continually fitted and tweaked until perfect.

The window from that initial conversation to delivery is months, not weeks, and if there is a lot of detailed specialist beading or embroidery work it can be significantly longer. I've had the great privilege of visiting Broderies Vermont, one of the beading and embroidery ateliers in Paris, and the complexity of the techniques and the skill of the artisans was extraordinary. It's a long process, but the end point is a bespoke garment that you will have for a lifetime.'

– CATHIE REID

MADE-TO-MEASURE

Customer appointments at atelier salons are limited and often booked out in advance of the collections even being shown. These appointments are not just the height of bespoke service for the incredibly discerning clientele, they're also required by law in order for a piece to be designated true haute couture.

It is during these private fittings that couture's made-to-measure benefits really shine and the client's relationship with the piece is born. Clients are led through the tailoring process by the designer, the premiere or a fitter, one of the senior atelier staff trusted to manage the process of making minute adjustments to get the correct size and shape.

Fit and comfort is of the utmost importance, but to a certain degree so is taste. Many royal clients, for example, will modify pieces to align with dress codes. Maria Grazia Chiuri's Spring-Summer 2019 couture collection for Dior was almost entirely black but at the Dior atelier, the client can request more than just a modest hemline – they can choose their preferred colour as well. 'In the past, the creative director defined the house and the clients came,' Chiuri explained. 'Now couture is an experience where the clients come to build a one-of-a-kind experience. You can decide the shape. You can decide the material.'

The rules for fittings at each house are different. Some, like Dior, insist on a minimum of three in-person appointments for each piece. At others, regular clients can rely on a custom mannequin, sculpted exactly to her body so that measurements and adjustments can be done while she's not there.

In all cases, though, pieces are entirely customised and with all the intricacies can take up to a year to produce. It is the perfect antidote to fast fashion.

'COUTURE CAN'T BE RUSHED, BUT THE *creation* TIME AND THE *experience* IS PART OF EACH GARMENT'S UNIQUE STORY.'

– CATHIE REID

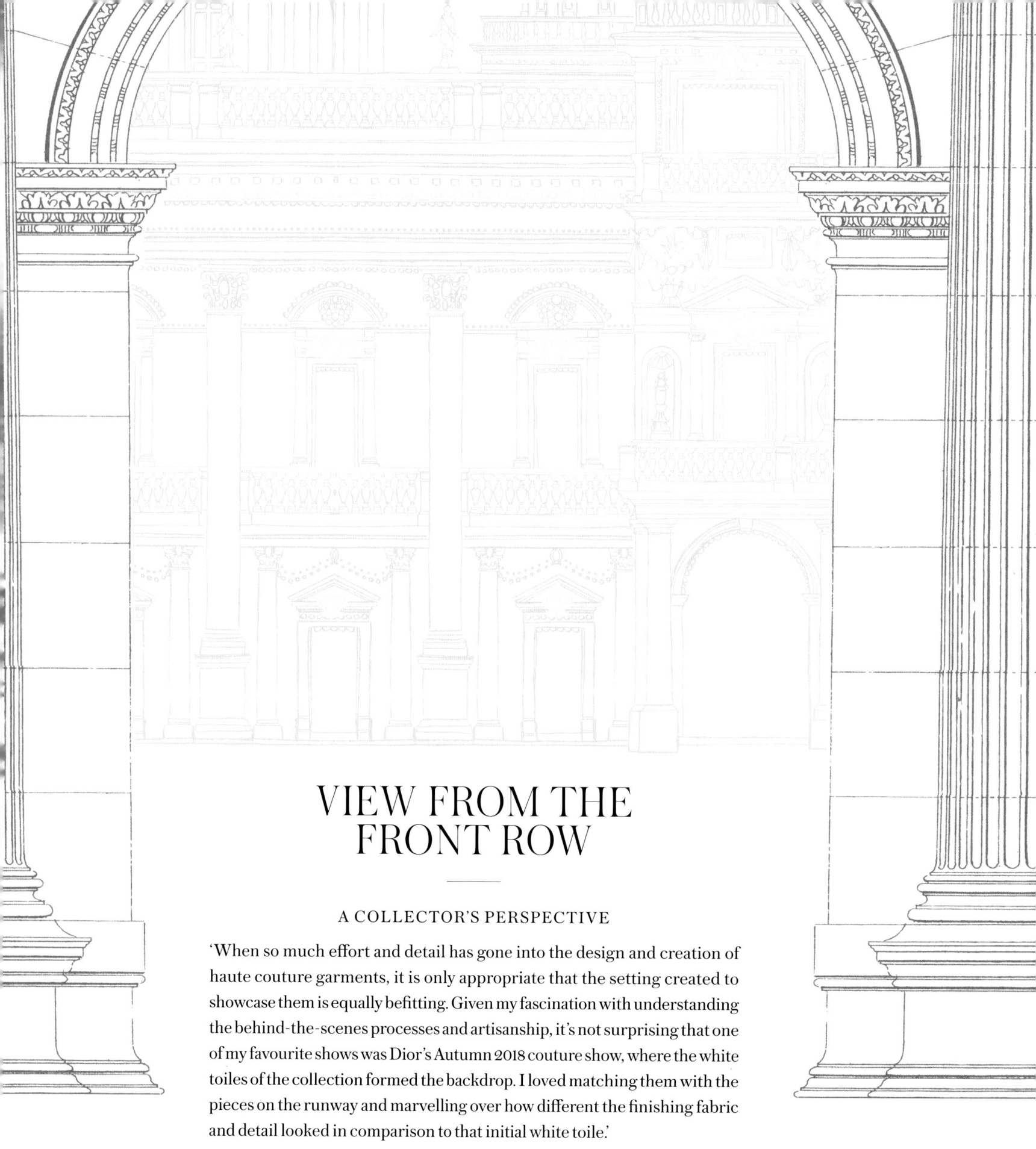

VIEW FROM THE FRONT ROW

A COLLECTOR'S PERSPECTIVE

'When so much effort and detail has gone into the design and creation of haute couture garments, it is only appropriate that the setting created to showcase them is equally befitting. Given my fascination with understanding the behind-the-scenes processes and artisanship, it's not surprising that one of my favourite shows was Dior's Autumn 2018 couture show, where the white toiles of the collection formed the backdrop. I loved matching them with the pieces on the runway and marvelling over how different the finishing fabric and detail looked in comparison to that initial white toile.'

– CATHIE REID

A WORLD OF POSSIBILITIES

Even in the tradition-bound realm of couture, things are changing and a new brand of clientele is emerging. Once the domain of the European elite, the couture clientele now spans the Middle East, China and Russia.

Women from the Gulf states – Saudi Arabia, Kuwait, Qatar and the UAE – are the largest buyers of couture today. The social calendars of the affluent in these countries are full of lavish parties and glamorous weddings where guests – sometimes 4000 at the one event – are divided into male and female rooms. I once sketched at a royal wedding in the Middle East and it was an incredible sight to see. The women's room was filled with guests dripping in amazing haute couture. With some Arab wedding celebrations lasting many days and requiring many different dresses, it's no wonder couture designers are in such demand in that part of the world.

A NEW TRADITION

In reflection of the global clientele, Dior took their first couture show to Dubai in 2019. They showcased their Spring-Summer collection in Al Safa park, which they transformed into a circus tent that mirrored the couture show put on in Paris only a few months earlier. The show, inspired by Christian Dior's renowned love of the Cirque d'Hiver, featured fifteen new designs exclusive to the Middle East region. The tent-like silhouettes, ruffled collars and bonnets from the Paris collection remained, but the new looks were paired with jewelled veils, bedazzled tights and a distinctly Middle Eastern colour palette. It was the perfect signal that an industry once so focused on the French capital is shifting its attention to cities further afield.

And it's not just the shows that are going global. These days, personal fittings are no longer limited to the ateliers. Many designers now travel to their clients, bringing with them racks of clothes to be fitted in hotel rooms or private residences all over the world. If you can't imagine ever checking such valuable dresses into the luggage hold, you're not alone: as Karl Lagerfeld told *WWD* in 2013, private jets are part of the changing face of fashion, helping to securely transport collections around the world.

ROYAL PATRONS

Few people can dream of owning even a single piece of couture, but take a look inside a royal wardrobe and you're sure to find an enviable collection. The first ever haute couture house, the House of Worth, was founded by the official dressmaker to Empress Eugenie of France, and royal families have been hugely important patrons for the artform ever since.

Princess Diana and Grace Kelly were both known to adore Christian Dior's classically feminine work. Queen Rania of Jordan is another royal whose couture wardrobe is to die for. She's long been a supporter of Elie Saab and wears his regal designs to many a state visit and official engagement. His long flowing gowns and opulent colour palettes are perfect for a queen. She also favours Givenchy and Dior. Where better to wear these incredible creations than a palace?

WORKS OF ART

A COLLECTOR'S PERSPECTIVE

'In my eyes the couture pieces I collect are like paintings or sculptures. The added bonus is that you can wear them too! I never buy anything that I don't intend to wear, but I quite often have pieces that I love on display in my bedroom for extended periods of time purely for the pleasure looking at them brings me. I store the pieces that are delicate, beaded or otherwise fragile offsite in a facility designed for art storage, where they have the space and expertise to ensure they are best preserved – which reinforces that they are in fact artworks!'

– CATHIE REID

'THE COUTURE PIECES I COLLECT REQUIRE *just* AS MUCH VISION, TALENT AND SKILL TO EXECUTE AS MORE TRADITIONAL *artistic* FORMATS.'

– CATHIE REID

STYLE NEVER GOES OUT OF FASHION

If you can't quite justify a custom-made piece from a Parisian atelier or a personal visit from a couturier in a private jet, one of the most fun and accessible ways to collect couture is going in search of vintage.

I am endlessly delighted by how well true couture stands the test of time – sometimes becoming all the more beautiful because of its story. I just love rummaging through racks of silk and sequins in the hope that I'll find a long-lost piece of fashion history, whether it's at the treasure troves of Parisian flea markets or the curated boutiques and auction houses.

I'm not the only one who sees the romance of couture from eras past. There are some serious vintage collectors out there who snap up rare and valuable pieces from auction houses like Christie's and Kerry Taylor Auction House in London or boutiques like William Vintage, owned by prominent collector William Banks-Blaney.

Hamish Bowles, international editor at large for *Vogue*, is another prominent vintage couture collector with an intimate understanding of the history of each piece he collects and what it represents. Bowles not only collects the garments, but also sources original couture sketches and photographs.

If a piece is in good shape, shows an important moment in a designer's career or has appeared in an iconic photograph, it will be all the more sought after by these dedicated fashion historians. That *Breakfast at Tiffany's* dress that first sparked my interest in couture? It was sold at Christie's in 2006 for over £400,000 with all proceeds going to charity.

FEATURE DESIGNER

Ralph & Russo

GUEST MEMBER CHAMBRE SYNDICALE DE LA HAUTE COUTURE SINCE 2014
40 PARK STREET, LONDON

Before Ralph & Russo were invited onto the official schedule at Paris couture week in 2014, it had been nearly a hundred years since a British designer had made it onto the esteemed list. And while the British like to claim the couple behind their most luxurious fashion house as their own – their atelier *is* one of the only haute couture houses based in London – Tamara Ralph and Michael Russo are actually from Australia. And their story of couture success is also one of hopeless romance.

The duo met in a chance encounter on the streets of London in 2005 and before long had fallen in love and become partners in both business and life. The motivations behind their fledgling design house's aesthetic were simple but genuine: 'There's no product I wouldn't wear myself – if there's something I see that I wouldn't wear, it won't get made,' Ralph told *Grazia* in 2018. And with this as their guiding force they took the couture world by storm, creating fairytale gowns beloved by brides and celebrities alike.

Even by their own admission, Ralph & Russo's rise has been stunningly quick. They opened a small atelier in a seven-floor, nineteenth-century townhouse in London's Mayfair district in 2010, and were invited onto the Chambre Syndicale's official schedule just four years later. They'd never even put on a runway show before their first show at Paris Fashion Week.

RALPH & RUSSO

TIMELESS ELEGANCE

While they might be one of the newest houses on the schedule and are often touted as one of the modernising forces in couture, Ralph & Russo are also deeply respectful of its traditions and craftsmanship.

Tamara Ralph comes from a long line of couturiers and learned the art of sewing from her grandmother, who ran ateliers in London before moving to Australia. 'My grandmother was always especially strict and would have me unpick an entire piece if one stitch was wrong – I think it was her way of triumphing over for me for the years of raiding her pattern archive!' she told *Harper's Bazaar*.

Ralph & Russo employs over two hundred artisans, almost four times more than at Dior's couture ateliers, and they have started an apprenticeship program to ensure that skills are passed down through many more generations to come.

With this respect for tradition in mind, the Ralph & Russo aesthetic is one of timeless elegance with a youthful touch. Classic and flattering, every single item in their collections is designed to be worn – beautiful rather than cutting edge. Hallmarks of their couture collections are feminine 1950s silhouettes and romantic dresses embellished with crystal-glass beading, pearls and sequins. With their penchant for A-line skirts, luxurious fabrics and muted tones, it's not surprising that a large portion of their couture work is for bridal clients.

THE PERSONAL TOUCH

'We cater for clients who travel constantly, know exactly what they want and rarely think twice about making a purchase.'

– TAMARA RALPH

Ralph & Russo are known for their intimate client relationships and an ethos that some have called 'personalised luxury'. Clients have direct access to Tamara Ralph and can order garments from her. She describes her clientele as 'extended family' and, when it comes time for fittings, sits down with each one personally to discuss their requirements.

Chapter
03
———

THE
DRAMA

The allure of fashion is never just about the clothes, and the value of haute couture isn't just in the intricate details and outstanding quality. It's also about the theatre and showmanship.

Twice a year when I see the couture events at fashion week I am entranced by the way that designers tell a story through spectacle. The very best shows on the couture schedule make an impact that is far greater than just the clothes. Designers like Viktor&Rolf, John Galliano and Alexander McQueen use the runway to convey deeper messages – often at a scale that would rival a Broadway show.

Beyond the runways, there are the lavish events attended by Hollywood stars and famous faces. The relationships between designers and the celebrities they dress are things of legend. The most famous of all were Givenchy and Hepburn, Yves Saint Laurent and Catherine Deneuve, but designers today still covet the drama of the A-list party. The red carpet is the alternative runway, after all, and for many designers it is as important as their couture shows as a way of showcasing collections.

'I live in total unreality, while being a down-to-earth designer.'
— KARL LAGERFELD

UNDER THE DOME

Each year, Chanel shows collections at the Grand Palais, one of the most iconic buildings at the very heart of Paris, and each year the historic building is completely transformed with the most elaborate sets. Any event under the gorgeous Art Nouveau dome is sure to be breathtaking, but with every show the set designers at Chanel seem to outdo themselves.

Some of my favourites have to be the Alpine winter wonderland 'Chalet Gardenia' Autumn-Winter 2019, and the reconstructed beach of Spring-Summer 2019, complete with beach huts and real lapping waves. There was also the life-sized rocket of Autumn-Winter 2018 that appeared to blast off halfway through the show. And who could forget the nine-metre-high iceberg, imported all the way from Sweden, that melted onto the floor during the epic Autumn-Winter 2010 show?

One of the most delightful sets was surely the Brasserie Chanel, where the Grand Palais was transformed into a luxe Parisian café. Models walked in, flung their coats over the backs of chairs and ate and drank at the bar. The best seats in the house for audience members were, of course, the red leather booths complete with Chanel croissants and coffee.

FOUNTAINS AND FORTRESSES

Never one for predictability, master of drama Karl Lagerfeld has also done some incredible shows for Fendi. One of the most breathtaking was the 'Legends and Fairytales' Autumn-Winter couture show on top of Trevi Fountain in Rome to celebrate ninety years of Fendi in 2016.

The sight of top supermodels gliding across a glass runway suspended above the fountain was unforgettable. It was the first and only time a fashion show has been allowed on the iconic landmark, and guests were flown to the event on a private Fendi plane from Paris to see the forty-six captivating ensembles.

At the end of the show, Karl tossed a coin into the fountain, as is tradition, but it was a much more substantial donation that had made the spectacle possible. Lagerfeld and Fendi funded a €2.2 million restoration of the fountain in the decade before, more than earning them the right to use the beloved cultural icon as a backdrop.

If you think a show on the Trevi Fountain can't be topped, Lagerfeld is also responsible for sending models down what has to be the longest runway in history: the Great Wall of China. The centuries-old landmark played host to a dedicated Autumn-Winter collection for Fendi in 2007. It took over a year to get the Chinese government to approve the location for the show, but it was definitely worth the wait to see models walking the runway at sunset.

'TO DO THIS ON A CRYSTAL BRIDGE OVER THE MOST FAMOUS FOUNTAIN IN THE WORLD? IF THAT'S *not a fairytale*, I DON'T KNOW WHAT A FAIRYTALE IS.'

– KARL LAGERFELD

THE COLOSSEUM TURNS RED

Couture parties can be just as spectacular as the runway shows. For Valentino's forty-fifth anniversary celebrations, a team of 1400 people were employed to put on one of the most elaborate parties the Italian capital has ever seen.

It seemed all of Rome was involved in the celebration: the Museum of the Ara Pacis staged a retrospective exhibition, Valentino collections were displayed on the streets lining the River Tiber, and at the Temple of Venus, overlooking the Colosseum, a dinner was held for thousands of guests with no expense spared. Silk napkins and tablecloths were embroidered in India with Valentino designs, 3400 glasses were ordered in Valentino's favourite yellow crystal, and 3400 plates were made in Italy to exactly his specifications.

The Chambre Syndicale de la Haute Couture even finished Paris Fashion Week a day early so that guests wouldn't have scheduling clashes to attend!

The most dramatic flourish of all came when the Colosseum was lit up entirely in Valentino red, fireworks were let off and models floated in mid-air, suspended on invisible threads. 'You know, for my Roman comeback, I have done the essence of my couture,' Valentino said. 'Very beautiful cocktail dresses. Very glamorous evening gowns. Very small red dresses. Glamorous. Glamorous. Glamorous.'

FEATURE DESIGNER

Alexander McQueen

FIRST COUTURE SHOW FOR GIVENCHY IN 1997
76–78 CLERKENWELL ROAD, LONDON

Late British designer Lee Alexander McQueen was known for causing a stir with his shows: both for his own label and for Givenchy, where he was creative director from 1996 to 2001. Like Lagerfeld with his elaborate sets, McQueen loved an immersive location, but where Lagerfeld awed with romance and fantasy, McQueen's talent for theatre was all about the macabre and subversive. He made the most exquisite garments then paired them with visionary performance art that shocked and awed.

McQueen started each collection with an idea or concept of what the runway show would be. The resulting collections were usually resplendent with dark fantasies and recurring motifs from nature or anatomy. While most McQueen collections weren't strictly couture, his clothes always had an unmistakably couture spirit. His technical knowledge was legendary, and his atelier staff knew that if they couldn't work out how to execute one of his designs, the master himself would make it happen. 'He was coming in every day, draping and cutting,' his successor Sarah Burton once told *Vogue* of his habit of resolving impossible challenges of fit and form.

WOLVES AND FIRE

A candlelit church, a warehouse for street-cleaning trucks and underground vaults below the streets of Paris were just a few of the unusual places to which audiences were lured for McQueen's runways. McQueen sent models onto a burning runway in a show inspired by Joan of Arc, and another time had models walk live wolves.

His iconic 'Voss' Spring-Summer 2001 show was inspired by a Joel-Peter Witkin photograph entitled 'Sanitarium'. It started over an hour late, with the audience forced to look at reflections of themselves in a giant mirrored box on the runway, and it ended dramatically when that same glass box, now holding a reclining naked model attached to a breathing tube and surrounded by live insects, shattered, releasing the insects into the air.

For his Spring-Summer 1999 show, Aimee Mullins, a double amputee and Paralympic athlete, walked for McQueen wearing a pair of custom-made prosthetic legs designed by the house. That same show ended with one of the most iconic performances in fashion: Shalom Harlow standing on a slowly revolving platform, flailing her arms while two Fiat robots sprayed her white dress with black, green and yellow paint.

McQueen dressed women to empower them. It was a theme that ran through all his couture collections, with their skull motifs and feathered layers. His ground-breaking shows left people stunned, amazed and sometimes horrified, but they were never without extraordinary creative vision.

'I KNOW I'M *provocative*. YOU DON'T HAVE TO LIKE IT, BUT YOU HAVE TO *acknowledge it.*'

– ALEXANDER MCQUEEN

LIGHTS, CAMERA, FASHION

Celebrity-filled red carpets and black-tie extravaganzas double as platforms for couture designers to create one-of-a-kind pieces and reach new audiences. I have been lucky enough to work at some of these events, and I'll never forget being asked to sketch at the Chopard Cannes Film Festival launch party in particular. I remember thinking I would never again see that much breathtaking couture all in the one place.

I am always secretly delighted by the behind-the-scenes drama of the red carpet – the cars on standby to drive guests just metres from their hotels so they don't ruin a faultless look, the crews of assistants helping manoeuvre enormous gowns through doorways and up staircases, and the mob of paparazzi all waiting to take the perfect snap. Every aspect of it is utter magic.

THE MET GALA

Outside of Paris Fashion Week, the most creative night on the couture calendar is surely the Met Gala. Hosted on the first Monday in May, the invitation-only party is a fundraising event for the museum's fashion department, the Costume Institute. Anna Wintour, editor-in-chief of *Vogue*, is the chair of the event and she oversees a carefully curated guest list as well as the dress code each year.

It's most certainly not the event for understated elegance. Designers can have fun, knowing the right look will get them in the headlines, and the very best guests are the ones that go all out and embrace the theme. Rihanna's show-stopping yellow fur cape in 2015, equal parts regal and dramatic, launched Chinese couturier Guo Pei into the global spotlight. Practically unknown to the Western fashion set beforehand, Pei was on everyone's lips in the weeks after the gala. It's no coincidence she was invited onto the official couture schedule only a few years later.

CANNES FILM FESTIVAL

Over the other side of the Atlantic, the screenings at Cannes Film Festival also play a special role on the couture calendar. The festival has a notoriously strict dress code and even the paparazzi that line the red carpets wear tuxedoes. For designers, the calibre of the red carpet at Cannes gives them a chance to showcase their craftsmanship and creativity to an extremely appreciative crowd. They know the images shot along the Boulevard de la Croisette will be sent around the globe. These are the moments dresses become iconic.

THE ACADEMY AWARDS

The red carpet at the Oscars is always awash with gorgeous couture. It is on this night of nights that the most classic of couture dresses are showcased, and so many Oscars looks are timeless testaments to style. The world still swoons over photographs of Grace Kelly in that ice-blue Edith Head gown from 1955 and Audrey Hepburn wearing white floral Givenchy in 1954. But the Oscars have also been home to some incredible modern couture pieces. Gemma Chan in hot pink Valentino in 2019 and Lupita Nyong'o in pale blue Prada in 2014 are my bets for looks that will make the classic Oscars images of the future.

FEATURE DESIGNER

Valentino

MEMBER CHAMBRE SYNDICALE DE LA HAUTE COUTURE SINCE 1962
8 PLACE VENDÔME, PARIS

Valentino Garavani is such a couture icon that he is known by his first name, as befits a master who reigned supreme over Italian couture for nearly five decades. The great Valentino founded his atelier in 1959 aged just twenty-nine, inspired to create beautiful things by old Hollywood glamour and the stars of the silver screen.

Many pin Valentino's success on a fateful meeting a year later when the young designer shared a table at the Café de Paris in Rome with his future partner, in business and in life, Giancarlo Giammetti. Together, the two men built an empire, with Valentino taking the creative lead and Giancarlo taking care of everything else.

The pair put on their first couture show at Pitti Palace in Florence in 1962. The parade of distinctive red dresses was an instant success. 'Valentino red' – the colour of poppies – would become the maison's defining signature.

Valentino designs may not be radical but they remain constantly glamorous and ever beautiful. Structured bows, ruching and exquisite draping come together in meticulously created masterpieces, all designed with one thing in mind: elegance.

VALENTINO

VALENTINO-RED CARPET

*'It's very simple.
I try to make girls look sensational.'*
— VALENTINO GARAVANI

Valentino more than achieved his goal of dressing those famous Hollywood stars he once watched on the silver screen. He has been almost universally adored by dignitaries, royalty and socialites alike, and has dressed more stars walking the red carpet than any other designer. Sophia Loren, Elizabeth Taylor and Audrey Hepburn were fans, and Jacqueline Kennedy Onassis was a close friend.

Valentino himself also exudes the extravagance and opulence of a true couturier. If there's one thing you can say about him, it's that he knows the art of living well. Always dressed impeccably, he travels by private jet often accompanied by his six pugs. He and Giammetti own many homes: a house on Capri, a chalet at Gstaad, an apartment in Rome and a superyacht in the Mediterranean as well as his most famous home, Château de Wideville just outside Paris. All his residences are filled with art, lavish tableware and beautiful objects.

When Valentino threw a lavish party to celebrate his forty-fifth anniversary, many suspected he was close to retirement and wondered what would happen to the esteemed house without him at the helm. After all, who could possibly replace such an icon? Surely no single person was up to the challenge.

And they were right. Valentino announced his retirement not long after the anniversary extravaganza, and within a year *two* head designers were appointed to the task: Pierpaolo Piccioli and Maria Grazia Chiuri.

A COUTURE HOUSE OF TODAY

Since Maria Grazia Chiuri left to join Dior, Pierpaolo Piccioli has held the top job by himself, and he has ushered Valentino into the twenty-first century with an understated style.

While many things remain the same under Piccioli's direction – the commitment to beauty, appreciation of women and love of poetry, to name a few – others are significantly different. Piccioli values community and diversity over luxury, and his couture exudes an ease and modernity that distinguishes it from the opulence of the house's founder. Piccioli has said that he wants Valentino to be 'a couture house of today – to meld couture and street; to do t-shirts and opera coats with the same care'.

The new Valentino signatures are voluminous shapes and bold colours, and each Piccioli collection radiates with creative energy. One of his finest creations, a pink feathery dress from his Autumn-Winter 2018 couture collection, left even hardened fashion editors in teary-eyed awe. The show received a standing ovation – joined enthusiastically by Valentino himself, who was sitting proudly in the front row.

Chapter
04

THE
DETAILS

Once the curtain closes on fashion week, the fireworks are over and the trends have come and gone, it is the clothes that remain. If you're fortunate enough to have held a couture piece in your own hands or, luckier still, worn one, you'll understand the intricate details and the hours of work that go into every single element.

Even with pieces that at first seem unembellished and simple, there is so much more than meets the eye. One of the most incredible examples of this that I have ever seen is in the couture tweed that is the foundation of so many Chanel garments. Every single piece of thread in Chanel's couture tweed is hand selected then delicately woven into place with thousands of other threads, meaning no two pieces of fabric – and no two Chanel jackets – are the same.

Everything (and I mean everything) is done by hand in couture ateliers. Every fabric flower is individually cut and moulded. Every single bead is stitched with precision-perfect technique. Every layer of tulle is handled with the utmost care. It's not unusual for twenty expert creators to be working on the one garment at the one time – and that doesn't even include the métiers d'art, whose specialised skills are the beating heart of the industry.

Under the direction of Karl Lagerfeld, Chanel started to buy up many of the independent button makers, embroiderers, plumassiers and milliners that once filled the laneways of Paris but were becoming close to extinct. Lagerfeld was motivated by a deep affection for the artisans and a dream of preserving their knowledge and standards for generations to come. Every December since 2002, Chanel has put on a show dedicated to these creators. The métiers d'art collections put the spotlight on the exquisite craftsmanship that defines couture.

HAND PLEATING

The craftspeople at Atelier Lognon hand-pleat fabrics using techniques that haven't changed in a century. The petites mains send their fabrics to the Lognon workshop, where it is ironed completely flat then rolled into one of the thousands of origami-like cardboard patterns that have been drawn and folded by hand into intricate moulds. The moulds are set with steam, heat or weights before being left to cool and work their magic to create exquisite textural designs in the fabrics. It is a mesmerising process to watch.

The atelier has been in the Lognon family for four generations, since it was founded in 1853. It is not just the unique savoir faire that has been passed down through the family – some of the moulds they use today were created in the early 1900s.

EMBROIDERY

When it comes to beads and sequins, the world's best designers rely on the needlework expertise at Maison Lesage. They have been embroidering for couture clients for nearly a century, and the artisans that hold the tambour needles in their Paris workshop are trained in their craft for five to ten years.

Lesage became globally renowned under the leadership of master embroiderer François Lesage. The house has accumulated 150 years' worth of samples into an unbelievable archive. Over 70,000 designs are meticulously maintained in floor-to-ceiling boxes in a secure room in their workshop. Couture designers consult these archives to discover the craft's possibilities and take inspiration for their next collection.

Before he passed away in 2011, François Lesage collaborated with many couturiers. Designers trusted him not only to turn their dreams into reality, but to inspire designs himself. One of his most incredible pieces was a jacket made in collaboration with Yves Saint Laurent and inspired by Vincent van Gogh's Iris paintings. It used 250,000 sequins, 200,000 individually threaded pearls and 250 metres of ribbon. The embroidery alone took 770 hours to complete. And the embroidered leopard-print dress François did for Jean Paul Gaultier in 1998 has to be seen to be believed.

'FOR ME *couture* IS ABOUT THE HAND – PEOPLE WHO *give dignity* TO MATERIALS. IT'S NOT ABOUT HOW EXPENSIVE THE FABRICS ARE.'

– PIERPAOLO PICCIOLI

FEATHERS

At the end of the eighteenth century, there were twenty-five master plumassiers in Paris, painstakingly curling, cutting, bleaching, dyeing and painting feathers by hand before attaching them to shoes, dresses, bags and headpieces. Now, there's Eric Charles-Donatien, creative director of Maison Lemarié, who trained under the late André Lemarié. Founded in 1880, the Lemarié studio on the edge of the Marais was a little oasis, protected from the hands of time, filled with rare old feathers. The workshop has moved to more modern premises in recent years, but the traditions of perfection will always be there.

The process of working with feathers is as laborious as it is meticulous. Feathers are dyed and steamed to add volume, then sorted by size and quality – anything with an imperfection or blemish is out. Next, plumassiers shape each feather by hand, cutting and curling one by one to achieve the desired effect before they can be used on a garment.

LACE

Lace is possibly one of the most luxurious fabrics of all and the traditional lacemakers at Sophie Hallette train for years to become skilled in their craft. Lacemaking is a unique process that involves first hand-drafting a pattern based on the maison's extensive archives before creating the intricate but surprisingly strong fabric on a centuries-old Leavers machine. Hallette lace has been used by nearly every couturier in Europe, from Alexander McQueen to Oscar de la Renta, Chanel to Iris van Herpen.

BUTTONS

When I think of buttons, two fashion icons come to mind: Coco Chanel and Elsa Schiaparelli. It just so happens that the two women were arch rivals, both working in Paris in the 1920s.

Coco Chanel famously commissioned a new button design for each and every piece in a collection. It is a tradition that continues to this day, and the premier button makers at Maison Desrues spend their days moulding, stitching and carving by hand to ensure each simple but refined Chanel button is precision perfect.

By contrast, Schiaparelli was known for collaborating with surrealist painters and sculptors for her couture collections, and buttons were where she had the most fun. If you look at the distinctive whimsical fastenings on any vintage Schiaparelli – in the shape of a horse, maybe, or a butterfly – chances are you will be viewing a tiny Salvador Dalí or Jean Cocteau.

FEATURE DESIGNER

Chanel

MEMBER CHAMBRE SYNDICALE DE LA HAUTE COUTURE SINCE 1945
29 RUE CAMBON, PARIS

Gabrielle 'Coco' Chanel and her most famous successor, Karl Lagerfeld, are two of the most iconic couture creators of all time. Together they epitomise everything I love about couture. Coco, with her enduring icons and motifs, and Lagerfeld, with his deep love and affection for the artisans behind the scenes, have together created a legacy for Chanel that is evident in everything the house creates.

I've written so much about Gabrielle Chanel in the past, but I just can't get enough of her story. From humble beginnings, Chanel took on the elite world of fashion and absolutely revolutionised it. She shortened hemlines, freed women from restrictive corsets and created a silhouette that is still endlessly referenced. Chanel designed with the everyday needs of women in mind and in the process inspired effortless style. She also gave us the most enduring of chic outfits – a little black dress, ballet flats and a spritz of Chanel N°5 is as modern today as it ever was.

And what can one say about the inimitable Karl Lagerfeld? Lagerfeld loomed large over the world of couture fashion for so many decades and was creative director at Chanel for an era-defining thirty-six years. He was the master of incredible sets at the Grand Palais and was oh so recognisable in his dark glasses, white ponytail and black leather gloves. But beyond the theatrics of his own curated persona, he had unwavering respect for the quiet, dedicated traditions of couture. Lagerfeld revered the savoir faire of the artisans who worked behind the scenes to produce the collections he dreamed up and was committed to celebrating them at every opportunity.

THE ICONS

Throughout the decades, Chanel has used classic details to reference its history like no other house, with recurring motifs that hark back to the days when Gabrielle herself stood in her rue Cambon apartment taking inspiration from the objects around her. Each intricate detail found in a Chanel couture piece tells a tiny but perfectly compiled biography of its founder's life.

THE PEARLS

'I only like fake jewellery because it's provocative.' Though Gabrielle Chanel owned many pieces of enviably fine jewellery, she was rarely seen without loops of faux pearls around her neck – a theatrical choice that perfectly offset her understated clothes. With these pearls, she pioneered the idea that having fun with costume jewellery was acceptable and to this day you'll find pearls embellishing so much of Chanel couture.

THE LION

Gabrielle Chanel was a Leo and she identified strongly with the symbolic animal of her star sign. She surrounded herself with gold lion statues when she worked, and she escaped to Venice, the city of lions, to grieve when her lover Boy Capel died in a car accident. Take a close look at any Chanel couture collection and you're likely to find a tiny lion embellishing a jacket button or dangling from a bracelet. The king of the jungle is never far away with Chanel.

THE CAMELLIA

Why did Gabrielle Chanel first pin a white camellia to a dress in 1923? It could be because these blooms are perfectly symmetrical, or that they were classically worn on men's lapels as a sign of unity and refinement. It could be that they bloom in winter and never lose their leaves, or because they don't exude any fragrance that would interfere with a woman's chosen perfume. Whatever the reason for her attraction to this flower, Chanel rendered them in almost every material and on almost every kind of garment.

THE QUILTING

Whether it's a feature on a 2.55 bag, a vest or a pair of two-toned flats, diamond-patterned quilting or 'matelassé' has been a staple of the house since it was first introduced by Gabrielle Chanel herself in 1955. It was likely inspired by Chanel's love of riding as a young woman.

RECREATING HISTORY

When Lagerfeld passed away in 2019, it was Chanel's strong sense of history that paved the way for his successor. Virginie Viard, the first woman to lead the house since Gabrielle Chanel herself, worked alongside Lagerfeld for over three decades. She has been overseeing the couture collections at Chanel since 1997 and Lagerfeld himself once described her as his second pair of eyes.

When she took over as creative director, Viard immediately looked to the past for inspiration, embracing the house codes but infusing them with a modern attitude. The sets for her early shows recreated historic scenes from Chanel's life: the famous mirrored staircase in her atelier, a library styled to resemble the one in her rue Cambon apartment, and even the cloister garden of the orphanage where Coco spent six years as a child. And Viard's couture, while simpler and more stripped back than Lagerfeld's, references her predecessor's collections at every turn.

With such a strong foundation to play with, I just can't wait to see how Viard evolves the Chanel narrative.

'I AM A *fashion* PERSON, AND FASHION IS NOT ONLY ABOUT CLOTHES – IT'S ABOUT ALL KINDS OF *change*.'

– KARL LAGERFELD

Chapter
05
———

THE
CITIES

While the home of couture is and always will be Paris, it's a global phenomenon with vibrant and distinctly different scenes all over the world. Designers regularly stage couture shows in Milan, where the local fashion set is just as passionate as their French counterparts, and the metropolises of New York and London both have long and distinguished couture histories of their own. These four are, after all, the fashion capitals.

And in recent years, other centres of couture have been emerging. Houses take their collections on the road to far-flung cities and there is a burgeoning clientele in many of the Gulf states, in Russia and countries right across Asia. As the previously Eurocentric tradition flourishes in these new cities, it has been infused with a totally different character. The results, I have to say, are magnificent.

PARIS

The cobbled streets, swoon-worthy boutiques, and the promise of a hidden workshop behind every door: I'll never tire of Paris, especially during fashion week.

The city of love is the epicentre of couture for so many reasons. It is where couture was born and where haute couture is governed, but it is also the home of the traditions and craftspeople that keep it alive. This state-sanctioned dedication to fashion is what makes the standards so high, but I think it has also fostered a particular appetite for the new and creative. The couture audiences in Paris are receptive to innovation and designers know they can push boundaries.

I have seen some of the most experimental shows at couture week in Paris, such as Viktor&Rolf's Autumn 2017 show, where models donned giant doll heads and padded, quilt-like clothes. The audience seemed surprised, but at the same time accepted that it made perfect sense. You don't get that in any other city.

MILAN

With Italy's rich fashion history and masters such as Valentino and Fendi, it's no wonder that to be in Milan during fashion week is to be in the most glamourous city in the world.

Everywhere you look, stylish people with impeccable taste abound. From the gilded sidewalks of the Quadrilatero d'Oro district to the classic espresso bars and everywhere in between, you don't want to look anything but polished in this city.

Milan's fashion scene exudes passion – the audiences are passionate about couture, the Italian designers are passionate about their collections, and couture wearers are passionate about their pieces. When I think of couture in Milan I think of bold gowns and opulent fabrics, and I think of course about beautiful women. Italian fashion celebrates feminine beauty above all else and nowhere is that more evident than in Milan.

LONDON

There is a reason Tamara Ralph and Michael Russo decided to have the headquarters for Ralph & Russo in London. The British capital, with its distinctly royal influence and jet-setting population, has a couture audience like no other. To many, the quintessentially British approach to fashion is one steeped in quality, tradition and refinement. And in a way that's true – so much of the couture I see in London is understated, elegant and discreet. It is about luxurious tweeds, restrained tones and excellent craftsmanship.

But there is another thread that runs through British fashion that I also love. It's the thread that is alive with individualism – that matches the spirit of late couture icon Alexander McQueen. I feel it when I wander the streets of London, see a perfectly curated show at the V&A or hear about the next exciting young designer to emerge from the Central Saint Martins design program. London may not have an official couture schedule at its fashion week, but it is a city of couture in every other way.

NEW YORK

New York City, home of the fourth big fashion week, has a distinctly different fashion flavour again. I just adore the exhilarating contrast between the luxury houses of 5th Avenue, with their discreet separate entrances for couture clients and exceedingly good service for valued customers, and the bustling energy of the city outside.

New Yorkers have fun with their couture. Gowns and sneakers, a mix of different designers, high fashion paired with high street – it all works in New York. You never know what guests will be wearing in the front rows of New York Fashion Week but you know it will be fabulous.

FEATURE DESIGNER

Giambattista Valli

MEMBER CHAMBRE SYNDICALE DE LA HAUTE COUTURE SINCE 2011
30 RUE BOISSY D'ANGLAS, PARIS

Giambattista Valli's commitment to craftsmanship is unparalleled, even in the world of couture. Born in Rome, he did the first of his two apprenticeships under Italian fashion master Roberto Capucci in Italy before moving to Paris to work under couturier Emanuel Ungaro. Valli eventually became creative director with Emanuel Ungaro but always dreamt of opening his own maison d'haute couture. Rumour has it he turned down the creative director job at Valentino in order to realise this dream.

Valli started his ready-to-wear line in 2005 then debuted his first haute couture collection in Paris for Autumn-Winter 2011. He has since made a name for himself marrying the much-loved tradition of haute couture with a new-world attitude.

You can always tell when you're looking at a Giambattista Valli dress. His signature silhouette is absolutely unmissable: layer upon layer upon layer of ruffled tulle, a cinched waist and a high-low train.

FABULOUS PRECISION

'I see collections as chapters of a single book: the book of my obsessions. I don't care about being edgy, au courant or the flavour of the season. I want to create beautiful dresses, and that's what women come for.'

– GIAMBATTISTA VALLI

Valli's dresses use hundreds of metres of sorbet-coloured material and take seamstresses thousands of hours to construct. They are frivolous, frothy, floral and fabulous. One dress from his Spring-Summer 2018 collection used 350 metres of fabric. For comparison, the Eiffel Tower is 324 metres tall.

But for all the impossible volume and girlish confection Valli sends down the runway each season, there is always an equal measure of precision-sharp lines and serious cuts. The Italian-born, Paris-based designer is all about balance. Everything he does is a story of opposites: romance and hard edges, tradition and pop culture, femininity and toughness. His own uniform – head-to-toe black with a single string of freshwater pearls – epitomises that contrast.

Even Valli's atelier, hidden away in a seventeenth-century building in the Madeleine district of Paris, has been renovated with opposing forces in mind. On one side is an elaborate and decorative ode to the original baroque architecture, filled with ornate furnishings. The other is an empty, neutral studio with stark white walls and almost no furniture. According to Valli, the beautiful side is for thinking, the other is for working. In any case, the doors between the main showrooms have all been cut super-sized to accommodate his elaborate gowns.

VALLI GIRLS

Valli's clients are the youngest of the couture set: the new generation of high fashion, taking their cues from famous names who've worn his gowns to grace the red carpets at Cannes and the Academy Awards. You need to have confidence to embrace these edgy explosions of colour and fabric.

'THE HARDEST THING IN FASHION IS NOT TO BE KNOWN FOR A LOGO, BUT TO BE KNOWN FOR A *silhouette*.'

– GIAMBATTISTA VALLI

DUBAI

Dubai is a city that manages to put luxury and style at the centre of absolutely everything, but never at the expense of tradition and culture. Nowhere is this truer than in the way the Emirati city celebrates couture.

Women in Dubai know how to dress for an occasion. They might follow strict dress codes outside the bounds of any party, but the minute they walk through the door it's another world entirely. The couture I have seen at Emirati events has been nothing short of incredible. It's lavish, opulent and incredibly sleek, and all the more magical for its unexpected appearance. It's no wonder couture houses like Dior are taking note and designing collections with these women in mind.

BEIJING

The oh so elegant fashion sets from Beijing and Shanghai have a love affair with couture that is almost unrivalled, and they have been front-row fixtures at the European fashion shows for years. So much so, that in 2019 Pierpaolo Piccioli decided to take the show to them. The creative director at Valentino produced an entire couture collection dedicated to China and staged it in extravagant fashion at Beijing's Aman Summer Palace.

The adoring audience had flown in from all over the world for the show but there was no denying it was an unmistakable ode to the East. Valentino red was paired with stunning bright pinks and opulent gold in a series of looks that confirmed to the world that couture was no longer just for Europe.

Those in the know should not have been surprised, however, that Beijing was a new couture hotspot. This is the city that has given us Guo Pei, China's haute couture queen.

MOSCOW

If there was a prize for the most theatrical couture city, it would certainly go to Moscow. Russian women have turned getting dressed into an absolute artform – one they execute with their own delightful brand of confidence. I get absolutely swept up in the fun of it all whenever I'm among couture fans from Russia.

I'm not the only one who appreciates the Russian approach to high fashion. In 2010, Jean Paul Gaultier achieved a long-held dream when he presented an haute couture retrospective at a Moscow train station. I personally can't think of a better designer to revel in the Muscovite spirit of couture as performance.

FEATURE DESIGNER

Elie Saab

CORRESPONDENT MEMBER CHAMBRE SYNDICALE DE LA HAUTE COUTURE SINCE 2006
1 ROUNDABOUT CHAMPS ELYSÉES, PARIS

Flowing gowns in golden hues and jewel tones with a thigh-high split, intricate beading and stunning embroidered embellishments are what makes a dress distinctly Elie Saab. Elegant, daring and chic, with luxurious materials and romantic draping – these are gowns for a modern-day princess.

Some of Elie Saab's clients are actual royalty – like Queen Rania of Jordan, who wore one of Saab's gowns to her husband's coronation in 1999. But any woman is transformed into royalty by Saab's impossibly regal creations.

Beirut-born Saab says he grew up surrounded by beautiful women and that his desire to create clothes for his sister and mother is what led him to his signature refined aesthetic. He opened his first atelier in Lebanon in 1982 when he was just eighteen years old and, despite now being based in Paris, he maintains a close connection to his home country through a distinctly Middle Eastern vision. He keeps ateliers in Beirut, where many of his collections are hand-embroidered and hand-painted, and his gowns have been described by some as the perfect combination of European silhouettes and Middle Eastern detailing. I have to say, I agree.

Saab had been making clothes for his Arab clients for years before he was admitted onto the Chambre Syndicale's official schedule in 2006, but his first real taste of worldwide fame came in 2001 when Halle Berry wore his now-iconic sheer burgundy gown to accept her Oscar for *Monster's Ball*.

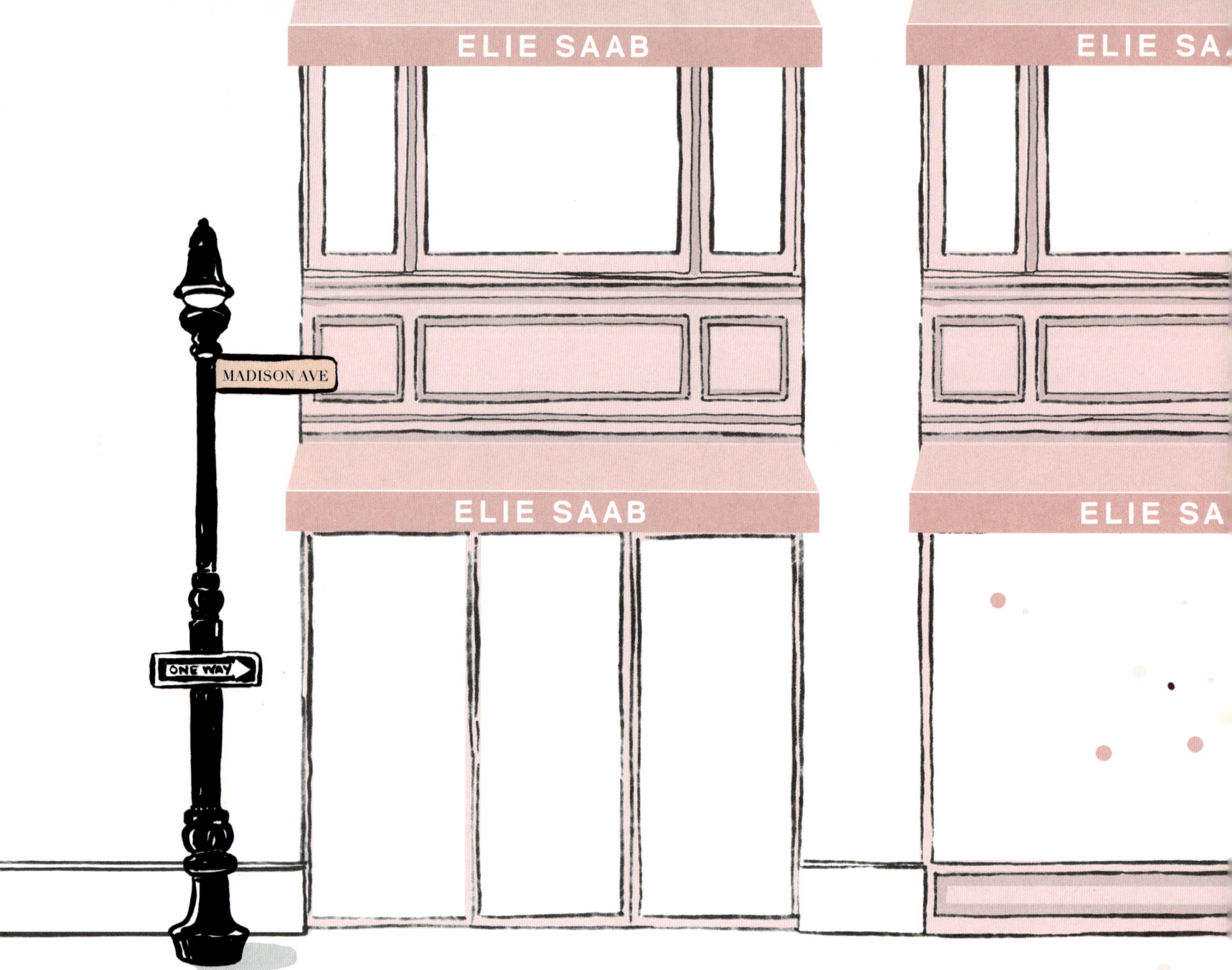

UNDERSTATED STYLE

There's no doubt Elie Saab has become one of fashion's most well-known names, but while other designers might court the spotlight, especially during the theatrics of fashion week, Saab barely makes it down the runway at the end of his own shows. In a world where drama queens reign supreme, he is reserved and understated. Saab maintains that it is the women he designs for who should be the centre of attention, not him. 'I wanted to express the brilliance and the glamour of women; I try to enhance their charm with my creations: I look at femininity with my utmost respect.'

'*Elegance* IS A STATEMENT, AN ATTITUDE. ELEGANT WOMEN ARE WOMEN OF CHARACTER WITH *confidence*.'

– ELIE SAAB

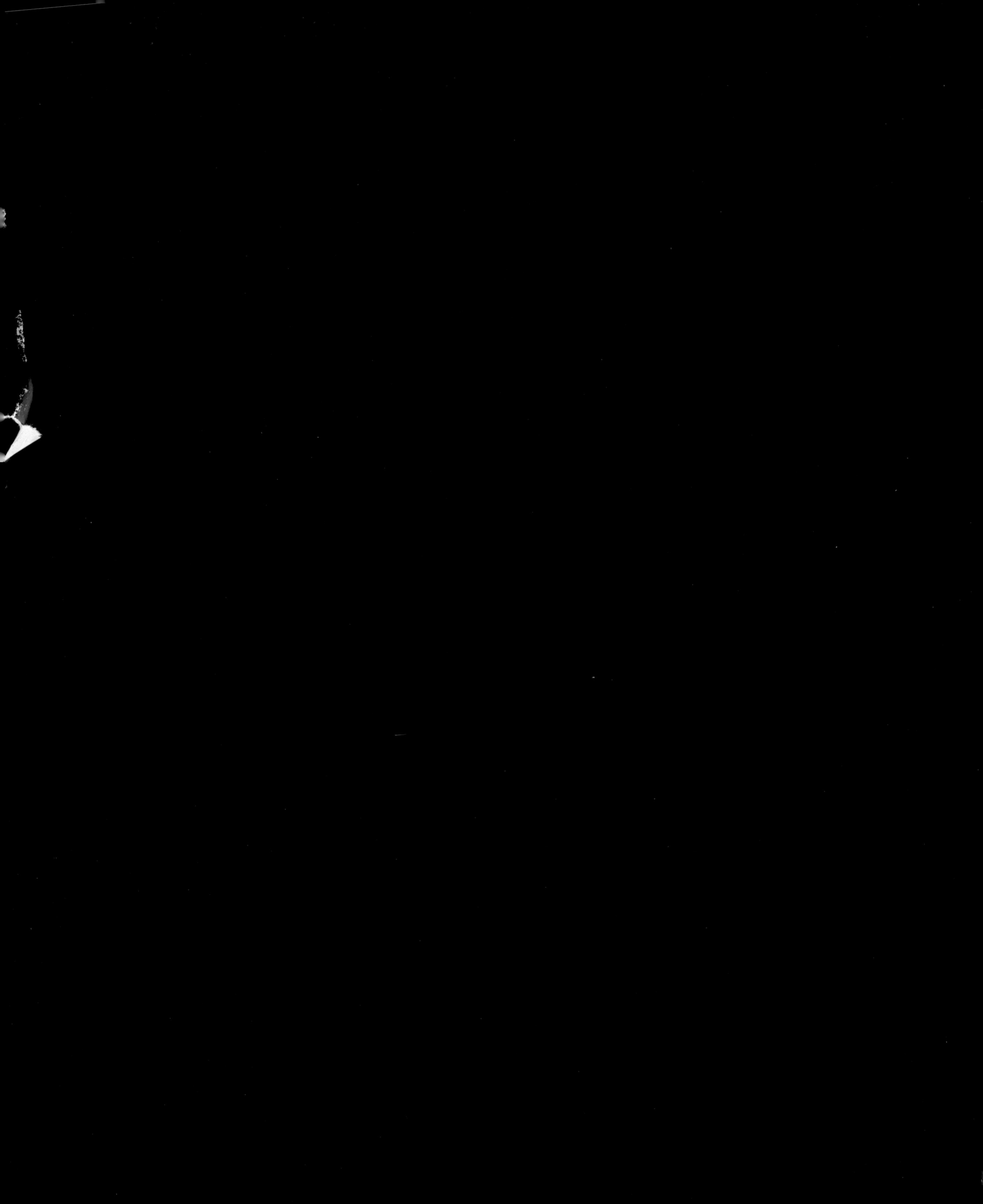

THE
INSPIRATION

Every artist has his or her muse, and the master creators of haute couture are no different. Sometimes creative influences are front and centre, like with Alexander McQueen's 'It's Only a Game' Spring-Summer 2005 collection, based quite clearly on the game of chess. Other times it's more abstract and cerebral, like Dior's ode to French surrealism for Spring 2018, or the piece in the Fendi retrospective after Lagerfeld's death that was inspired by a book on the Vienna Secession movement that Karl Lagerfeld had once gifted to the house.

But like with house codes and signatures that are repeated collection after collection, there are wider themes that designers right across the couture landscape keep revisiting. Look closely and you'll spot these central influences in nearly every season.

ROYALTY

Ever since the very first couture house was founded by the dressmaker to Empress Eugenie of France, so many couture clients have come from royalty. It therefore makes sense that couture designers consistently return to royalty as inspiration.

The lavish world of kings, queens and palaces provides such a rich creative pool to draw from: full gowns, striking necklines, bodices encrusted with jewels, not to mention a colour palette of ruby reds, jade greens and deep purples. Alexander McQueen's Autumn 2008 collection was royal inspired; Christian Dior famously took regular inspiration from Versailles, and John Galliano sent models down the runway in replica British royal crowns for a Dior couture show in 2004.

A TALE OF FALLEN KINGS

Elie Saab created a spectacular celebration of medieval queens in his 'Tale of Fallen Kings' Autumn-Winter 2017 collection. There were sparkling capes, jewel-toned velvets, fur stoles and full circle crowns aplenty on a runway decorated by embroidered royal banners. It was breathtakingly fantastical and contemporarily elegant.

THE EAST PALACE

Who could forget the impossibly regal Guo Pei fur-lined yellow cape that Rihanna wore at the 2015 Met Gala? Pei has made regal creations before, but she took her royal credentials up a notch in 2019 with her Spring-Summer collection titled 'East Palace', inspired by the ancient royal abodes of China. The looks were full of Eastern extravagance – long, trailing sleeves, ceremonial silk tunics, tasselled adornments, red and gold embroidery and beading for days.

BOTANICALS

If the quest for beauty is so central to couture, what better muse than a flower? Couture designers are constantly paying homage to the natural world.

Lagerfeld returned to this theme over and over, whether an ode to the gardens of Versailles, or his Fendi Autumn-Winter 2017 haute fourrure collection, where he took inspiration from the textures found on the forest floor and recreated them out of fur. Giambattista Valli found inspiration in the gardens of Paris's Parc de Bagatelle, Jardin du Luxembourg and Jardin des Tuileries for his 2016 couture show. And I'll never forget the incredible wisteria dresses he created for his Autumn 2014 collection. One of Alexander McQueen's most persistent motifs was the English rose – from some of his earliest collections to Sarah Burton's current designs. His Sarabande flower dress, made from fresh flowers, was a mesmerising highlight of the Spring-Summer 2007 collection.

FLOWERS AND TULLE

*'You can never really go wrong if you
take nature as an example.'*
– CHRISTIAN DIOR

Dior was famously inspired by gardens. 'I drew women-flowers, soft shoulders, fine waists like liana and wide skirts like corolla,' he said, when describing the designs of the New Look. He was himself an avid gardener and so many of his dresses had an overwhelmingly botanical influence.

One of the most incredible is a cocktail dress from his Spring 1952 couture collection. Each pink-and-yellow flower was created by hand by master embroiderer Rebé and stitched to the white silk organza with exacting placement – densest at the waist and then thinning as they fall to the hem – to replicate a meadow in spring. Gorgeous.

Dior's current creative director, Maria Grazia Chiuri, has drawn on the wealth of botanical forms and colours for the duration of her time at the house, with her first-ever Dior couture collection comprising dresses with hand-dyed silk petals pressed between layers of tulle.

NEW-AGE NATURE

Even avant-garde couture newcomer Iris van Herpen, whose work is so heavily influenced by new technologies and man-made structures, turns to nature to find inspiration for many of her collections. Her 'Wilderness Embodied' Spring-Summer 2018 collection took inspiration from how natural landscapes merge into urban and how water pools on the body.

'My Wilderness collection explores the wilderness that we as humans have inside us as well as the wilderness in nature,' she told *Dezeen*. The collection included 3D-printed shoes that look like tangled roots and a 'foliage dress' that took 260 hours to make.

FEATURE DESIGNER

Viktor & Rolf

CORRESPONDENT MEMBER CHAMBRE SYNDICALE DE LA HAUTE COUTURE SINCE 2013
HERENGRACHT 446, AMSTERDAM

For Dutch designers Viktor Horsting and Rolf Snoeren, the inspiration behind their collections is just as important as the clothes they produce. The famous duo's first foray into fashion was with a couture collection in 1993 and from the beginning their focus has been on concept above all else. 'The ultimate aim is expressing our ideas in the best way; to have people wearing it is a great bonus,' the designers told *The Independent*.

The pair took a break from couture in the early 2000s to focus on other projects but returned to the schedule in 2013. They now have a much larger commercial following, but their couture collections are still distinctly in line with their fashion-as-art philosophy. Theirs may not be the most accessible clothing but what it lacks in wearability, it more than makes up for with innovation and eccentricity.

ON THE WALL

Viktor&Rolf's 'Wearable Art' Autumn-Winter 2015 collection demonstrated their artistic commitment most explicitly. The dresses for the show began as framed artworks mounted on the wall, which Viktor and Rolf themselves then removed one by one and dressed the models in as they came down the runway.

This wasn't the last time the designers took centre stage during one of their shows. They have started shows by meditating on stage, and they were also on the runway to dress a model for their 'Russian Doll' collection in 1999. Maggie Rizer rotated on a dial like a ballerina on a music box as the pair dressed her in layer upon layer of clothes until she was wearing eight entire looks from the collection: seventy kilograms of couture.

Viktor&Rolf's Autumn-Winter 2014 couture collection 'Red Carpet Dressing' was made entirely out of ... red carpets. The collection was a comment on celebrity culture – in their words, 'a meditation on a contemporary obsession'.

LASER PRECISION

For all their conceptual shows and extremely structured pieces, both Viktor and Rolf have a true couturier's approach to craftsmanship. One of the most remarkable dresses from their 'Cutting Edge' collection of Spring-Summer 2010 is a gorgeous red tulle gown with huge holes laser-cut into it. It's a dramatic look from afar but look up close and you'll see a masterclass in precision detail and incredibly fine tailoring.

'FOR US A SHOW IS SOMEHOW A WAY OF *telling a story*. OF COURSE THE *clothes* ARE VERY IMPORTANT, BUT THE SHOW ITSELF SHOULD BE ITS OWN ENTITY.'

– ROLF SNOEREN

STORYBOOK FANTASIES

Couture is all about telling stories, so designers unsurprisingly return to magical myths and legends to inspire their collections. Maria Grazia Chiuri's first ever couture show for Dior, 'Labyrinth' Spring-Summer 2017, was held on a moss-covered set in the Musée Rodin, with jewels hanging from the branches of trees overhead. It came straight from a Hans Christian Anderson tale. The whimsical looks, worn by models that resembled like woodland nymphs, only confirmed the inspiration – Bar jackets with capes and hoods, evening dresses in delicate powdery colours, embroidered with stars and birds, and headpieces made from tree branches and feathers. There's never a shortage of spells to be cast in the magical world of couture.

TALES AS OLD AS TIME

Fendi's 'Legends and Fairytales' show on top of the Trevi Fountain was based on the work of Danish storybook illustrator Kay Nielsen. The collection was a testament to the intense workmanship of the petites mains toiling behind the scenes: dresses embroidered with scenes from fairy tales, hand-painted fabrics in pale pinks, creams and blues, microscopic squares of mink painstakingly stitched together to create mosaic-like forest scenes and floral appliques of hand-crafted fur. The illustrations of princesses, castles, majestic horses, flowers and owls with textured rococo embellishment were all inspired by Nielsen's illustrations of a 1914 fairytale collection, *East of the Sun and West of the Moon*.

THE FROG PRINCE

*'Life to me is a bit of a
Brothers Grimm fairytale.'*
– ALEXANDER MCQUEEN

Alexander McQueen took a more macabre approach to fairytales, aligned with the dark Brothers Grimm tales. McQueen was a masterful storyteller and there were plenty of magical narratives and themes in his collections over the years: girls in hoods walked wolves down the runway, humans became shapeshifters and mythical creatures abounded. 'The Girl Who Lived in the Tree', his Autumn-Winter 2008 collection, was inspired by a 600-year-old elm tree in his own backyard. The show told the story of a girl who climbs down from the tree to meet a prince and become a queen.

06 THE INSPIRATION

THE BRIDE

Some of the greatest couture creations of all time have been designed with a single bride in mind. In a custom that started in the 1940s and was followed by all couture houses for decades, the last look in any couture show would be bridal.

Yves Saint Laurent really took the custom to the next level with his 'cocoon bride' of 1965. The infamous knitted wedding dress was inspired by Russian nesting dolls and caused a sensation. It is still one of the most talked about bridal couture looks. These days, not all designers uphold the tradition, but Karl Lagerfeld famously kept it going to the very last for his Chanel brides. Jean Paul Gaultier flipped the custom on its head for his Spring 2015 couture show, sending bride after bride down the runway then closing the show with Naomi Campbell dressed as the bouquet. Her moss-green one-piece wrapped in cellophane with flowers poking out the top was Gaultier at his playful best.

THE *new guard*, THE YOUNG DESIGNERS AND MAKERS *breathing life* INTO THIS ARTFORM, ARE BUILDING ON THE *legacy* OF COUTURE WITH EVERY COLLECTION.

FEATURE DESIGNER

Jean Paul Gaultier

MEMBER CHAMBRE SYNDICALE DE LA HAUTE COUTURE SINCE 1997
325 RUE SAINT-MARTIN, PARIS

During his incredible fifty-year career, Jean Paul Gaultier shook the world of fashion to its core. The Parisian-born designer was a true showman who revelled in the spectacle of the runway and broke barriers wherever he could.

Gaultier, who showed his last couture collection in 2020, was always irreverent and fun. He founded his namesake label in 1982 and debuted his first couture collection in 1997. Every one of the forty couture collections since was a feast of wit and escapism.

Gaultier famously put Madonna in the now-iconic conical bra and was known as one of the earliest designers to play with gender norms, sending countless men down the runway in surprisingly masculine skirts. Dita Von Teese was a regular on his runways, and he once made a fashion editor levitate as part of a magic-themed show in 2006.

Gaultier's clothes, too, offered an escape from everyday life. They were often high camp and playful, and he had a definite subversive bent. He designed for different people and different body shapes and brought together many divergent ideas of beauty.

JEAN PAUL GAULTIER

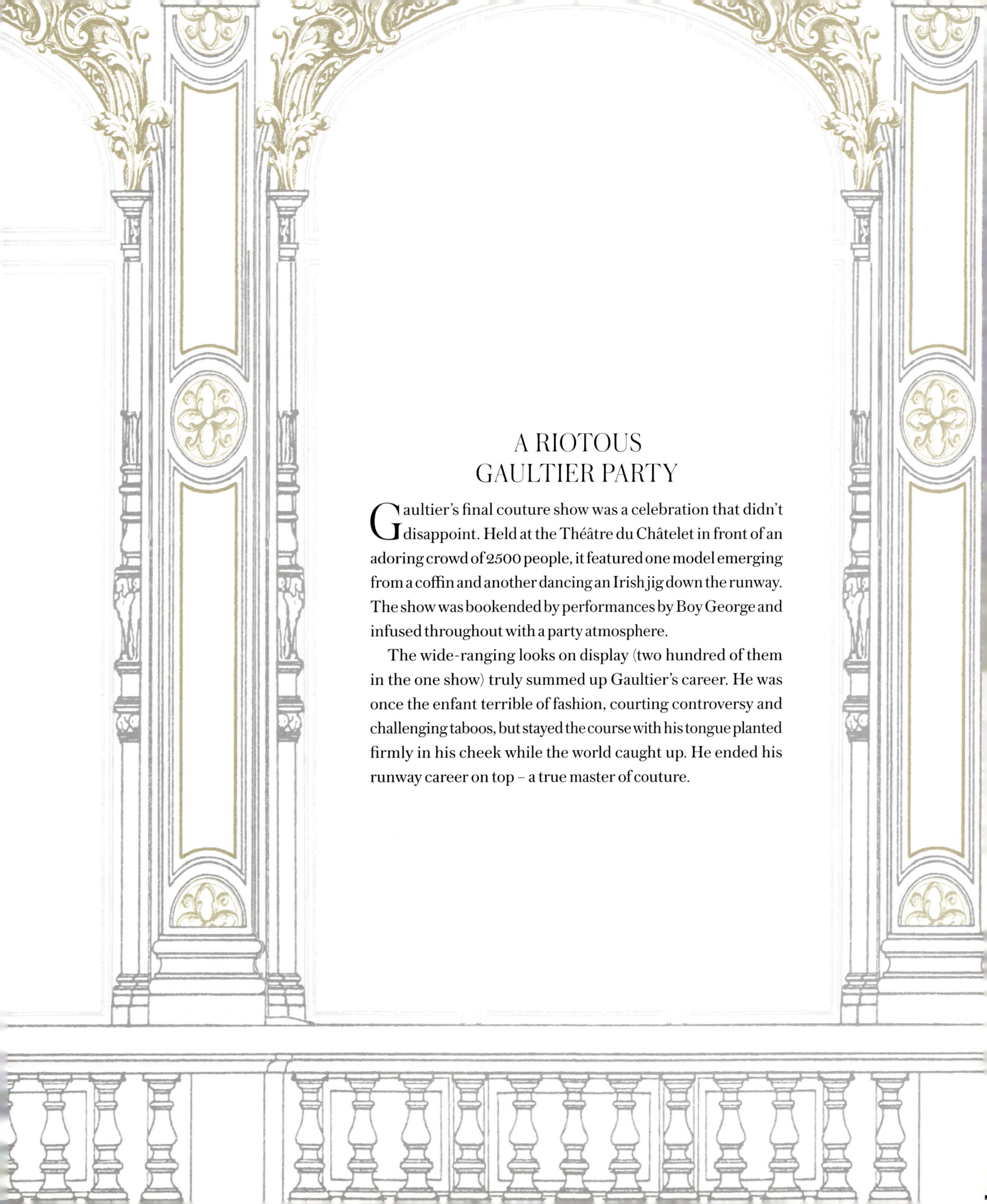

A RIOTOUS GAULTIER PARTY

Gaultier's final couture show was a celebration that didn't disappoint. Held at the Théâtre du Châtelet in front of an adoring crowd of 2500 people, it featured one model emerging from a coffin and another dancing an Irish jig down the runway. The show was bookended by performances by Boy George and infused throughout with a party atmosphere.

The wide-ranging looks on display (two hundred of them in the one show) truly summed up Gaultier's career. He was once the enfant terrible of fashion, courting controversy and challenging taboos, but stayed the course with his tongue planted firmly in his cheek while the world caught up. He ended his runway career on top – a true master of couture.

CODES OF COUTURE

Of all recurring motifs that can be found in the world of couture, Gaultier's are the most recognisable in popular culture. He had a code like no other: floor-length gowns made of denim, nautical stripes sewn from intricate feathers, lingerie as outerwear and so much leather. He also had a sense of humour and delighted in pairing high-fashion techniques with everyday themes. He rebelled against the stuffy traditions of couture while staying totally committed to the craftsmanship and techniques that are at its heart.

'THE SHOCK OF THE WAY I *mix* PATTERNS AND FABRICS CAN BE *disconcerting,* BUT WHAT I AM TRYING TO DO IS *provoke* NEW IDEAS.'

– JEAN PAUL GAULTIER

ACKNOWLEDGEMENTS

In many ways, this book is the one that I've always dreamed of creating.

A huge thank you to Emily Hart and Arwen Summers from my wonderful publishing house, Hardie Grant. Our eighth book together and the joy of working with you is even greater than when we first started.

To Martina Granolic, my partner in crime and all things fashion! Thank you for delving into the world of couture and seeking out every element that makes it so inspiring. Thank you for being by my side through every sketch, every show and every detail. I dedicated this book to you because without you, it wouldn't have been possible.

To Murray Batten, also our eighth book together! You are a dream to create with and your skill is unmatched by any other designer. Finally, we've created a big, bespoke book and I think this is your best design yet. Thank you for going on yet another creative journey with me.

To Andrea Davison, thank you for being so collaborative in your work. I loved your outlook on couture from the very first moment that we met. You found every single fascinating detail and brought it to life on the page.

To Todd Rechner, thank you for taking so much care and precision with all of my books, including this one. Of all the books we've worked on, this one is our most beautiful of all.

To Cathie Reid for sharing your inspiring stories as a collector of couture. I admire you enormously as both a businesswoman and as someone who so generously gives back to the world. If you ever tire of your couture pieces, I will happily look after them for you!

To Justine Clay, for seeing my potential in the very beginning and helping me navigate the world of becoming an artist.

To all the talented designers, thank you for giving me the privilege of working with you over the years and allowing me to be a tiny part of your incredible world.

And finally to my family, Craig, Gwyn and Will. Thank you for supporting my dreams and for always being ready to go on the next big adventure!

ABOUT THE AUTHOR

Megan Hess was destined to draw. An initial career in graphic design evolved into art direction for some of the world's leading advertising agencies and for Liberty London. In 2008, Megan illustrated Candace Bushnell's number-one-bestselling book *Sex and the City*. This catapulted Megan onto the world stage, and she began illustrating portraits for *The New York Times*, *Vogue Italia*, *Vanity Fair* and *TIME*, who described Megan's work as 'love at first sight'.

Today, Megan is one of the world's most sought-after fashion illustrators, with a client list that includes Givenchy, Tiffany & Co., Wedgwood, Louis Vuitton and *Harper's Bazaar*. Megan's iconic style has been used in global campaigns for Fendi, Prada, Cartier, Dior and Salvatore Ferragamo. She has illustrated live for fashion shows such as Fendi at Milan Fashion Week, Chopard at the 2019 Cannes Film Festival, Viktor&Rolf and Christian Dior Couture.

Megan has created a signature look for Bergdorf Goodman, New York, and a bespoke bag collection for Harrods of London. She has illustrated a series of portraits for Michelle Obama, as well as portraits for Gwyneth Paltrow, Cate Blanchett and Nicole Kidman. She is also the Global Artist in Residence for the prestigious Oetker Hotel Collection.

Megan illustrates all her work with a custom Montblanc pen that she affectionately calls 'Monty'.

Megan has written and illustrated seven bestselling fashion books: *Fashion House*, *The Dress*, *Coco Chanel*, *New York*, *Paris*, *Iconic* and *Elegance*. She has also written three books in her much-loved series for children, Claris the Chicest Mouse in Paris.

Visit Megan at meganhess.com

Published in 2020 by Hardie Grant Books,
an imprint of Hardie Grant Publishing

Hardie Grant Books (Melbourne)
Building 1, 658 Church Street
Richmond, Victoria 3121

Hardie Grant Books (London)
5th & 6th Floors
52–54 Southwark Street
London SE1 1UN

hardiegrantbooks.com

All rights reserved. No part of this publication may be reproduced, stored in a retrieval system or transmitted in any form by any means, electronic, mechanical, photocopying, recording or otherwise, without the prior written permission of the publishers and copyright holders.

The moral rights of the author have been asserted.

Copyright text and illustrations © Megan Hess PTY LTD 2020
Copyright design © Hardie Grant Publishing 2020

A catalogue record for this book is available from the National Library of Australia

The Illustrated World of Couture
ISBN 978 1 74379 444 9

10 9 8 7 6 5 4 3 2 1

Publisher: Arwen Summers
Project Editor: Emily Hart
Researcher: Andrea Davison
Design Manager: Jessica Lowe
Designer: Murray Batten
Production Manager: Todd Rechner
Production Coordinator: Mietta Yans

Colour reproduction by Splitting Image Colour Studio
Printed in China by Leo Paper Products LTD.

The paper this book is printed on is from certified FSC® certified forests and other sources. FSC® promotes environmentally responsible, socially beneficial and economically viable management of the world's forests.